Magical Mosaics Coloring Book
Flora and Fauna

original art by Geneviève Crabe

Amaryllis Creations
2015

Published by Amaryllis Creations
www.amarylliscreations.com

Introduction

Welcome! This is my second coloring book, and the first of a series of Magical Mosaics coloring books. The drawings contain hidden objects for you to find, and color in colors different from the background. You can see the whole process on the back cover.

About Colored Pencils

Colored pencils are a very versatile medium. Good quality pencils are highly pigmented and blendable. I use primarily Prismacolor pencils, which are wax based.

Have a light touch when you color; then you can apply several layers of color and create smooth blending and shading.

Although I have complete sets of pencils, I find that I always return to a small set of colors.

This is what I have in my portable set:

- Spanish Orange, Orange
- Permanent Red, Crimson Lake, Tuscan Red
- Light Aqua, Aquamarine, Cobalt Turquoise
- Light Cerulean Blue, Cerulean Blue, Indigo Blue
- Rose, Mulberry
- Lilac, Violet
- Limepeel, Olive Green, Dark Green
- Burnt Ochre. Chocolate, Dark Brown
- Back. White
- Cool Grey 20, 50, 70%
- Warm Grey 10, 20, 30, 50%
- French Grey 20, 50, 70%

Please note...

If you are going to color in the book, I recommend putting a sheet of card stock behind the page you are working on.

About Me

Following a thirty-year career in high-tech, I am now devoting my time to artistic pursuits. I am a digital artist, Certified Zentangle® Teacher, a teacher of bead embroidery. My book *How to Make 100 Embroidery Motifs* was published in January 2014, and my first coloring book, *Genevieve's Mandalas*, was published in October 2015.

If you have any questions, you can email me at gcrabe@mac.com.

My Other Products

- More coloring books.

- Geneviève's Mandala Stencils:
  a mandala design kit consists of several circular grid templates.

- Tangle organizers for Zentangle® artists.

- Digital art tutorials on YouTube.

- Brushes for the Procreate digital art app for iPad.

For the latest information, visit my website

www.amarylliscreations.com

Special thanks to Kelly Barone for the title idea.

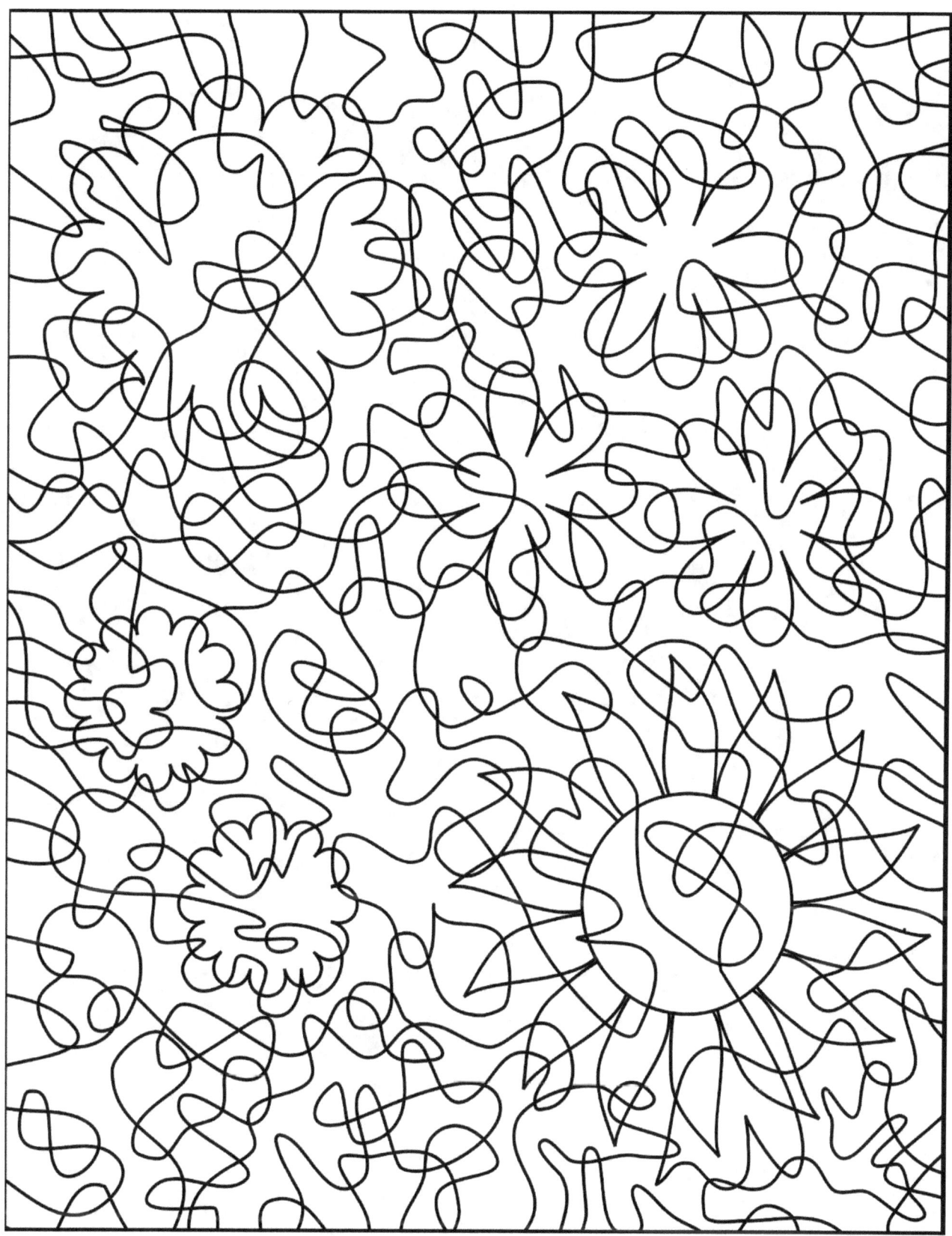

7 flowers

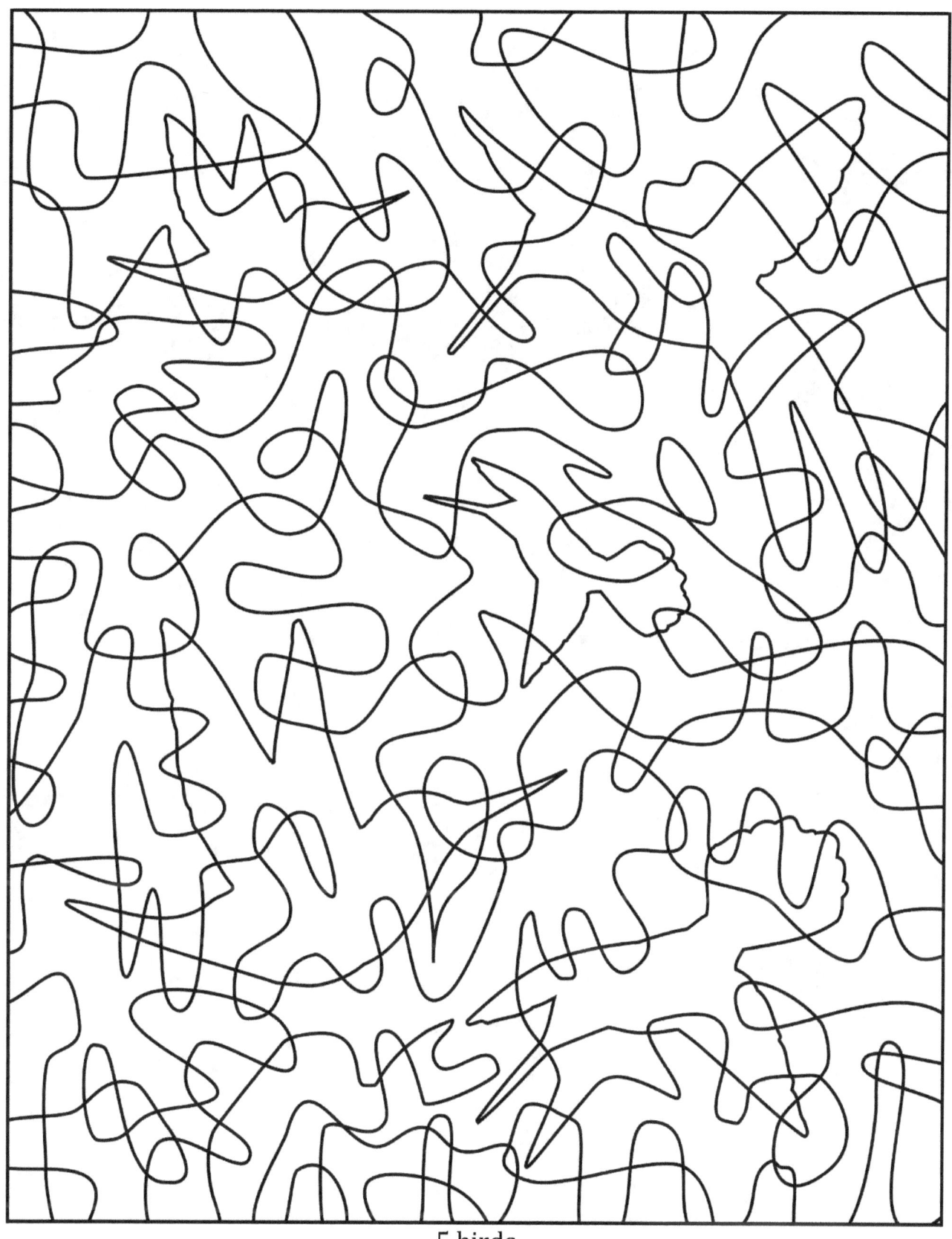

5 birds

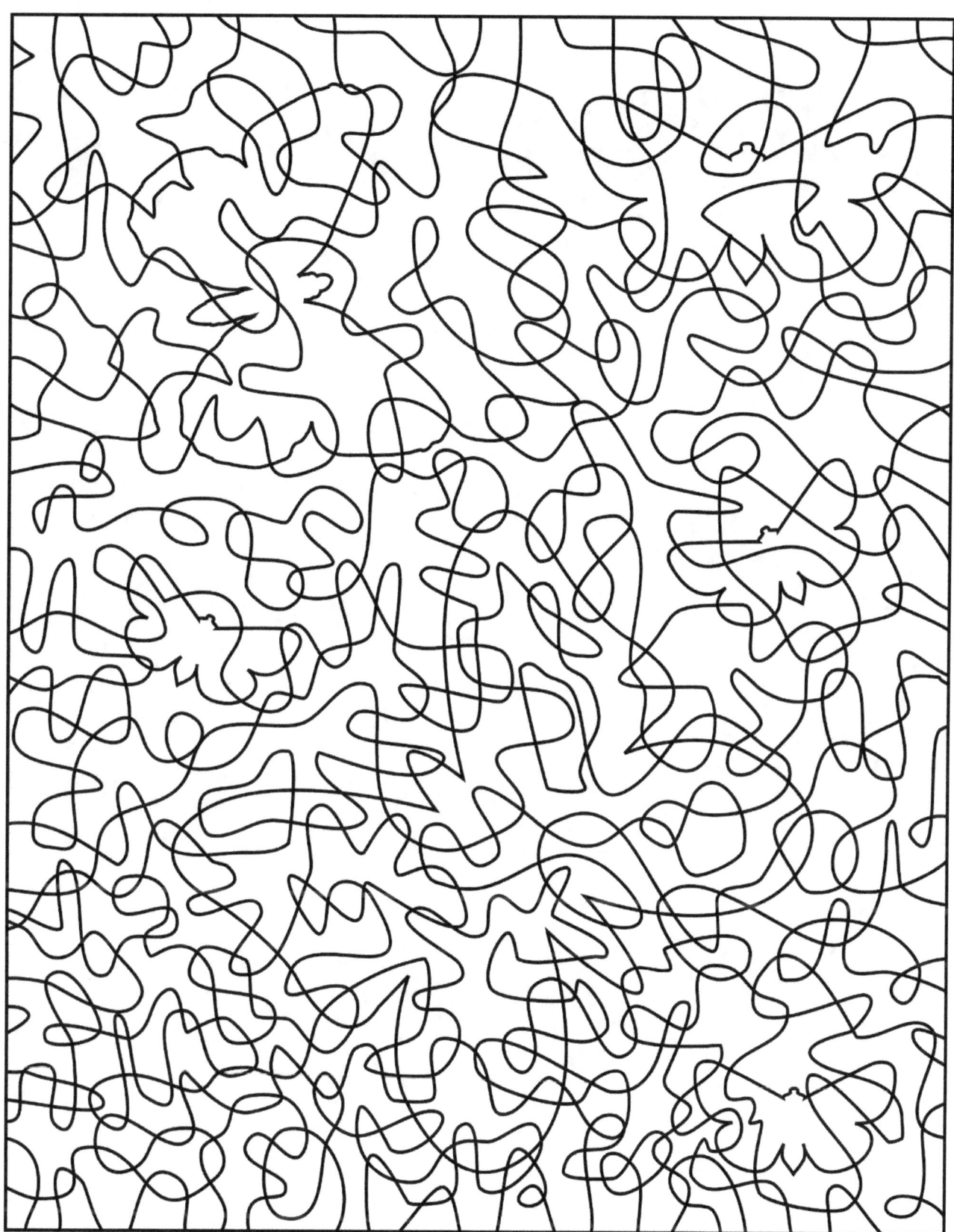

6 butterflies

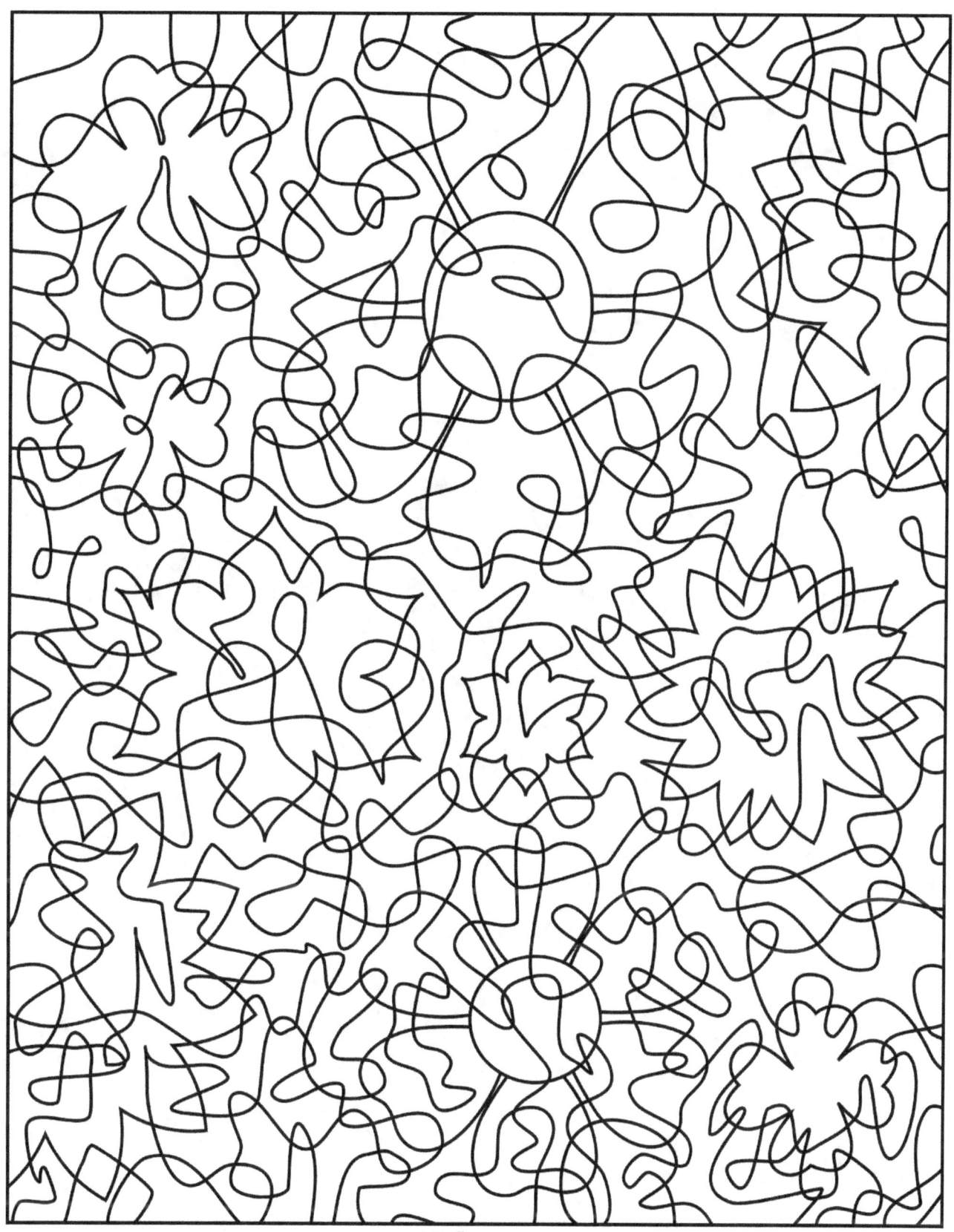

10 flowers

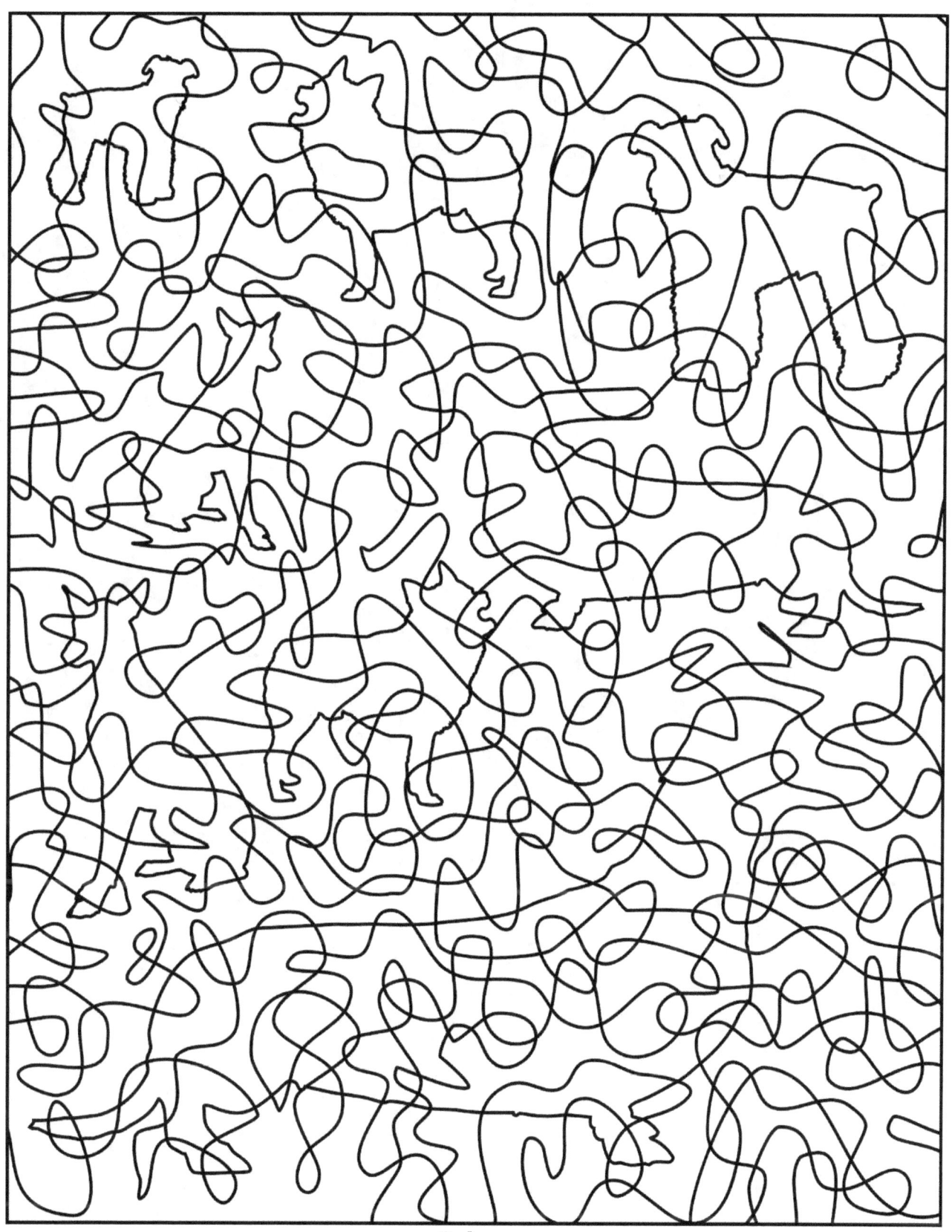

8 dogs

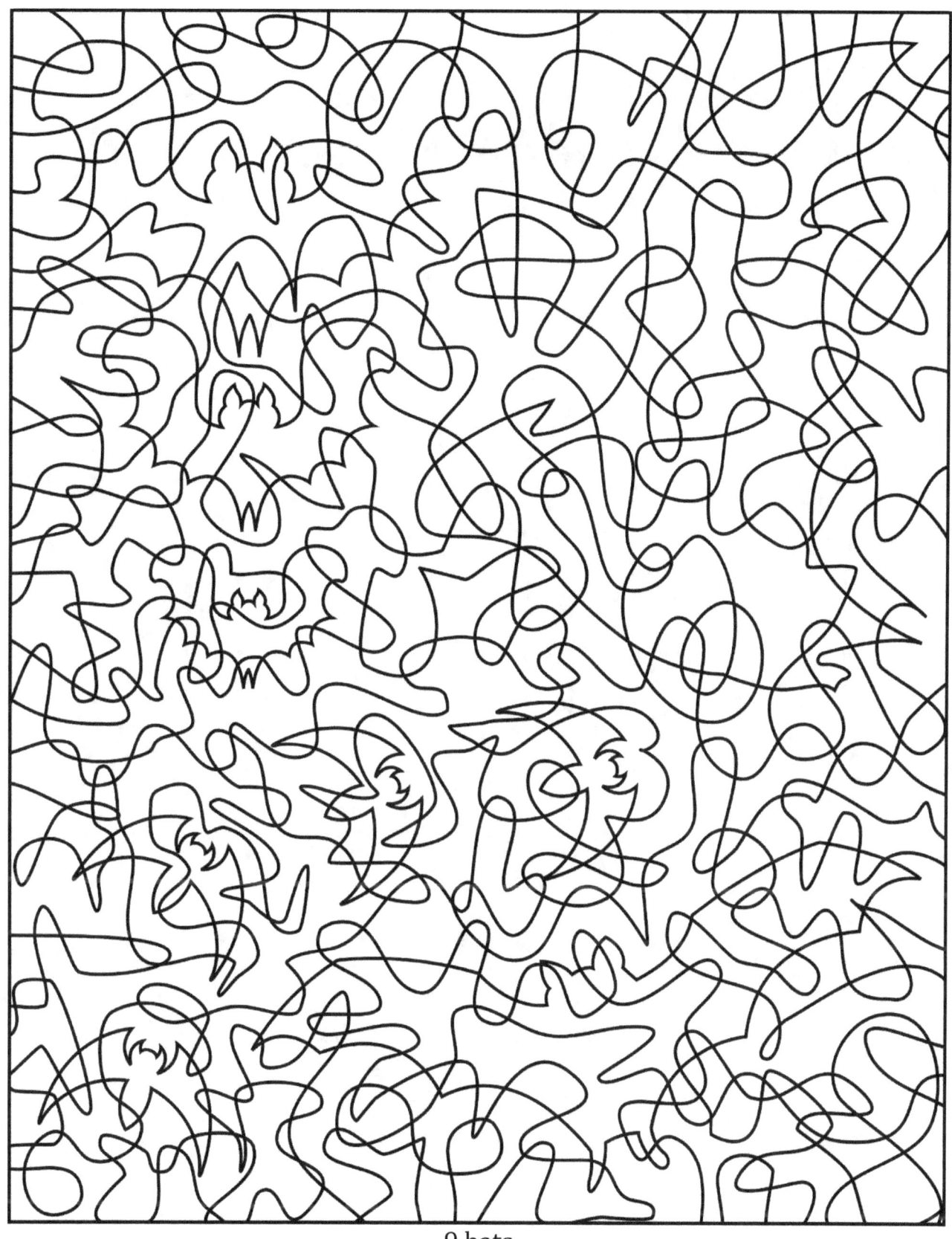

9 bats

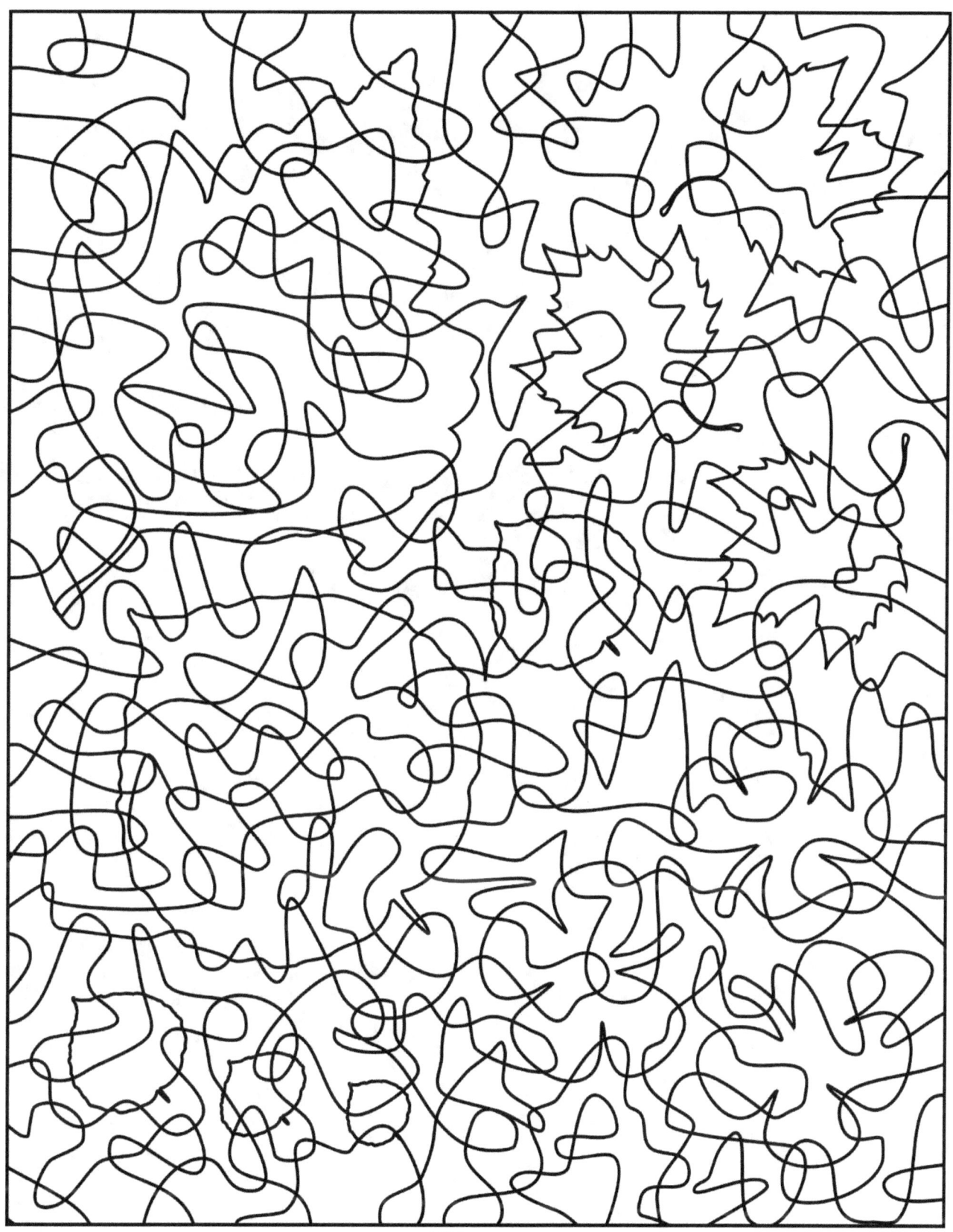

12 leaves

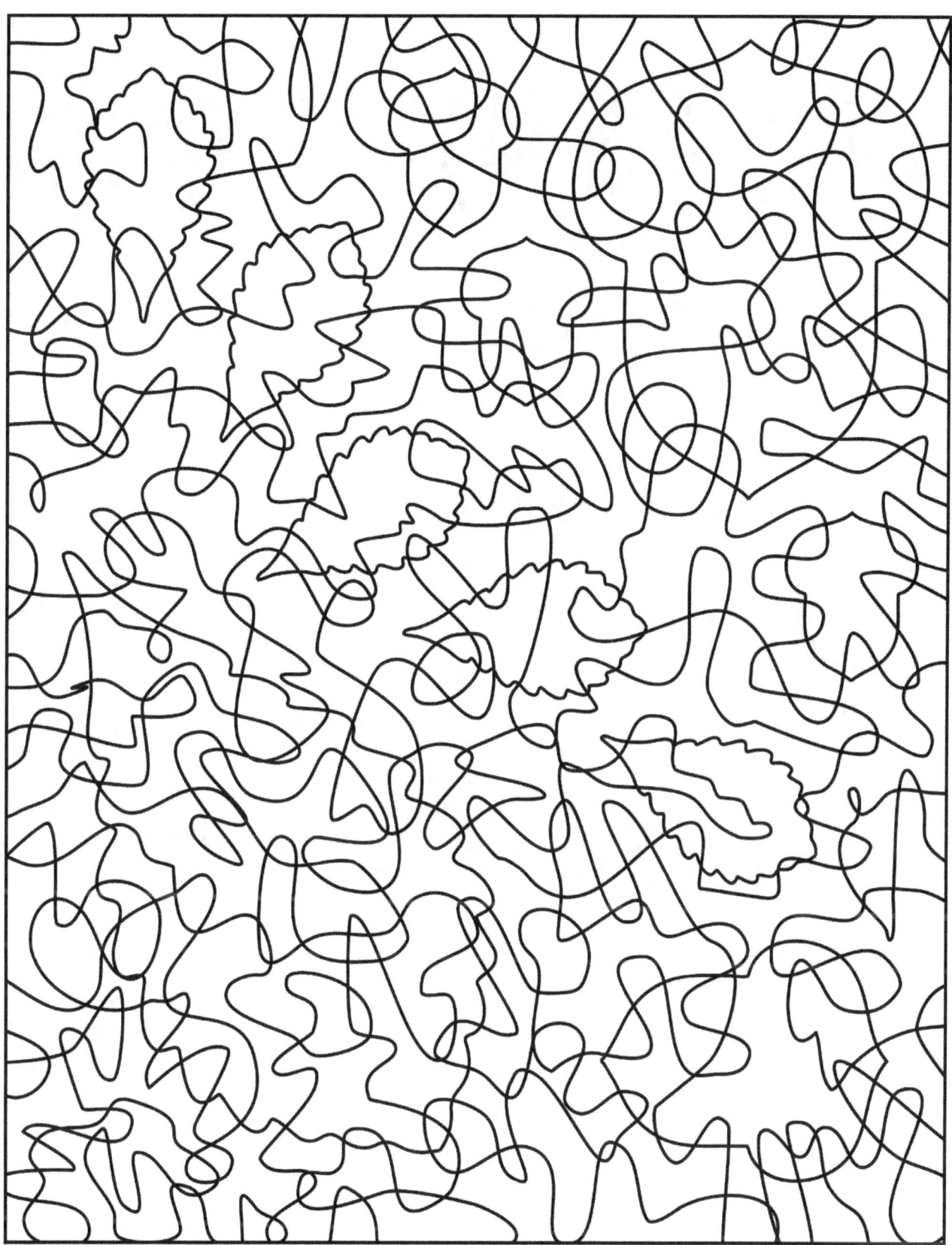

6 leaves, 5 acorns

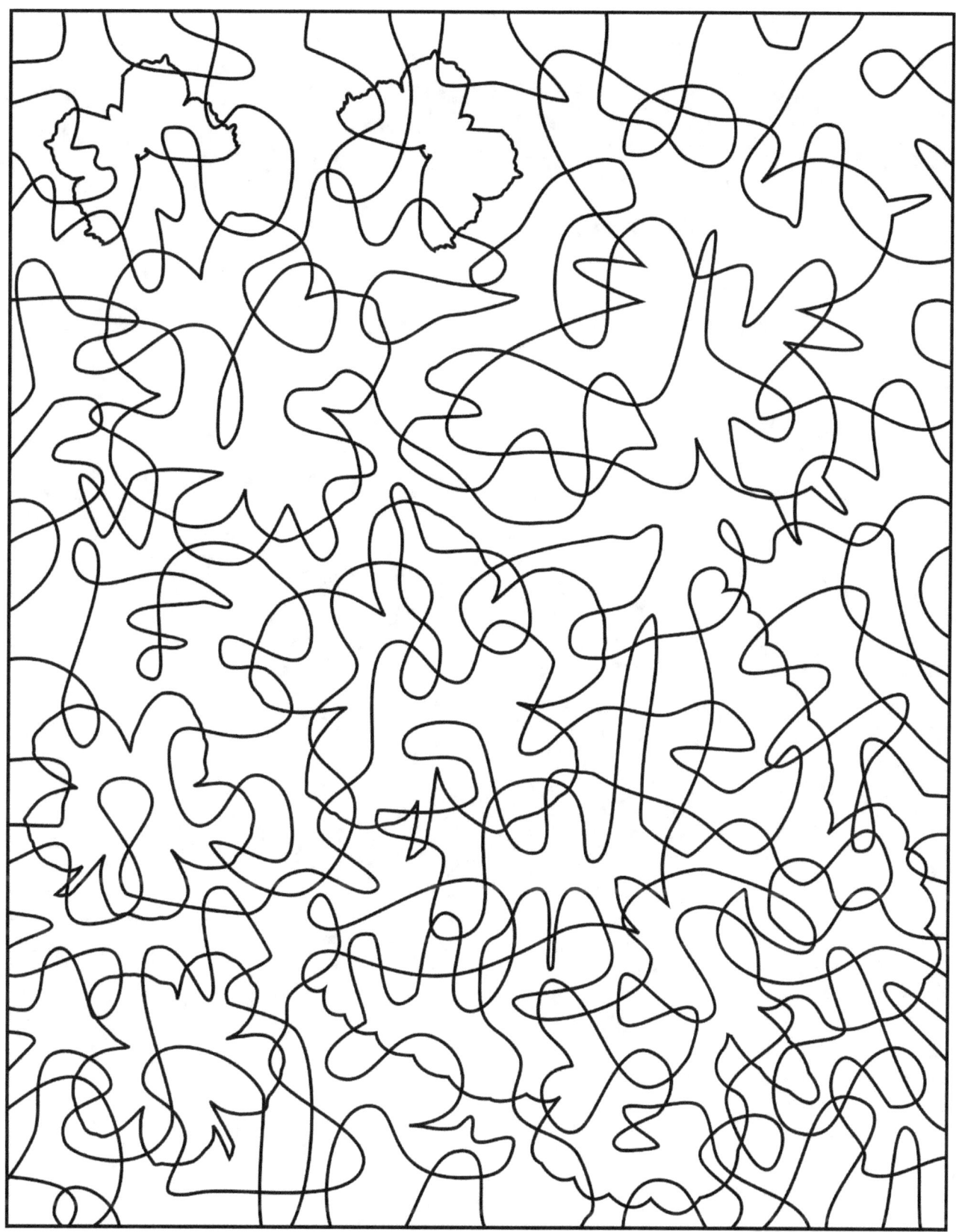

4 flowers, 4 butterflies

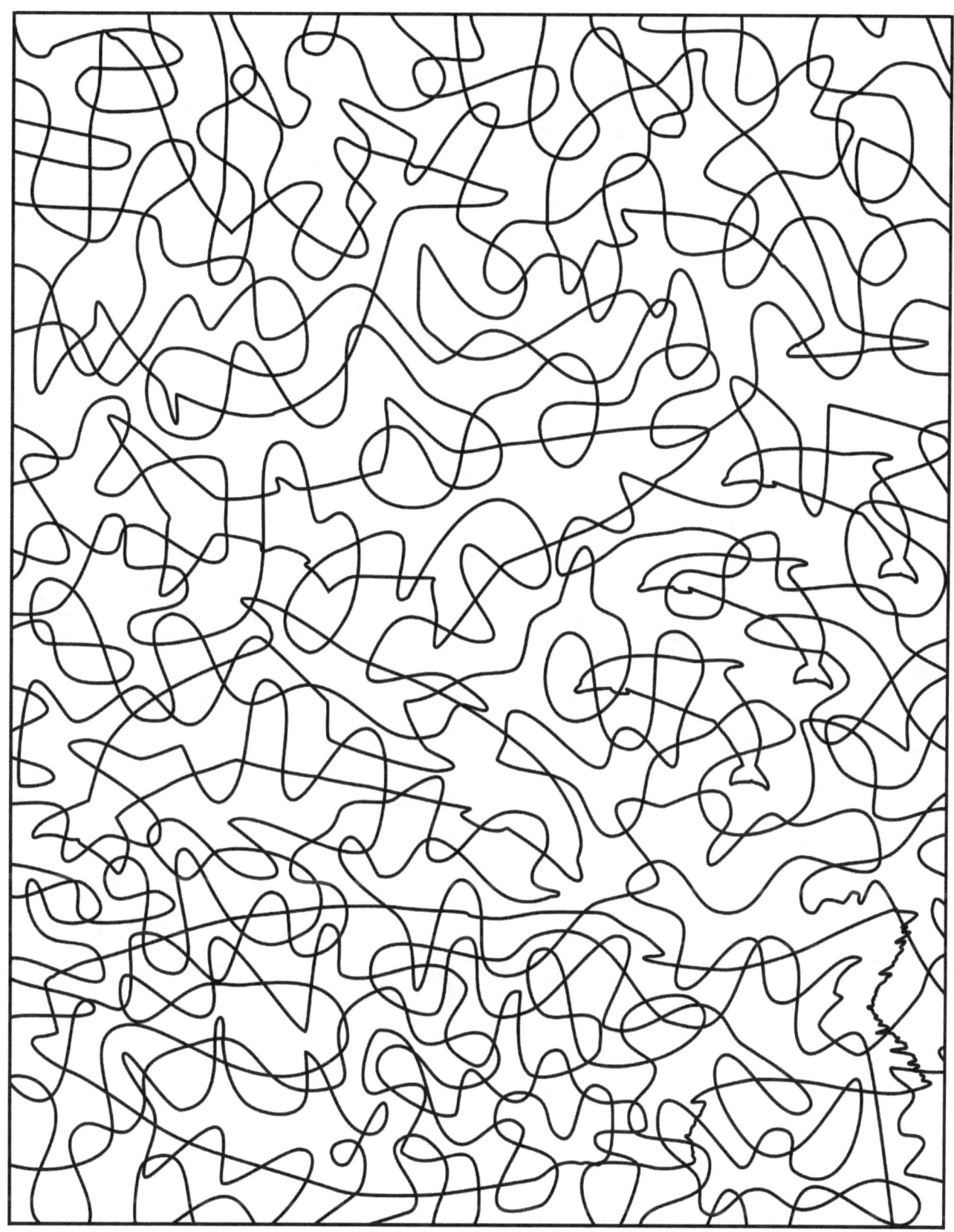

3 fish, 5 mammals

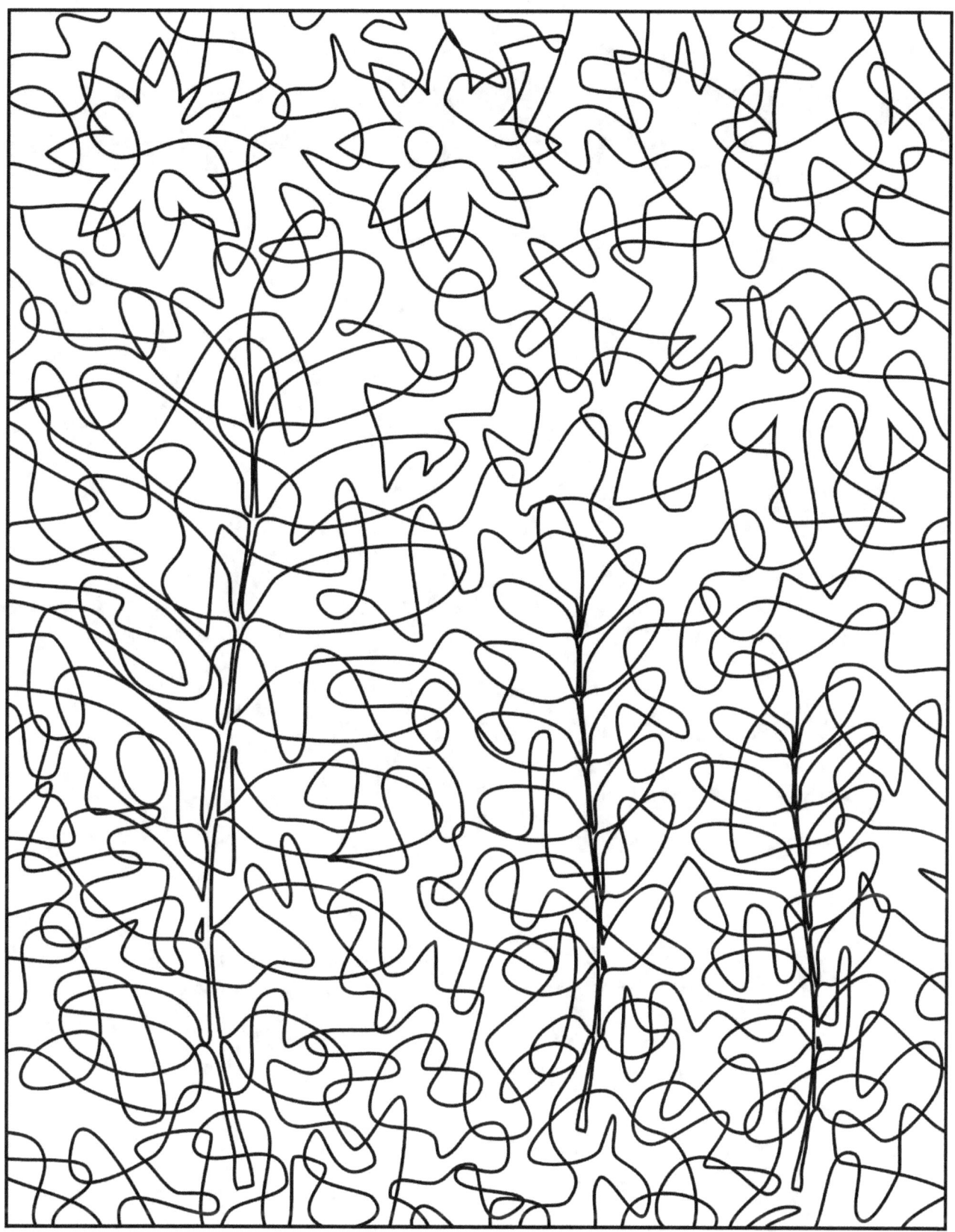

3 flowers, 3 leaf clusters

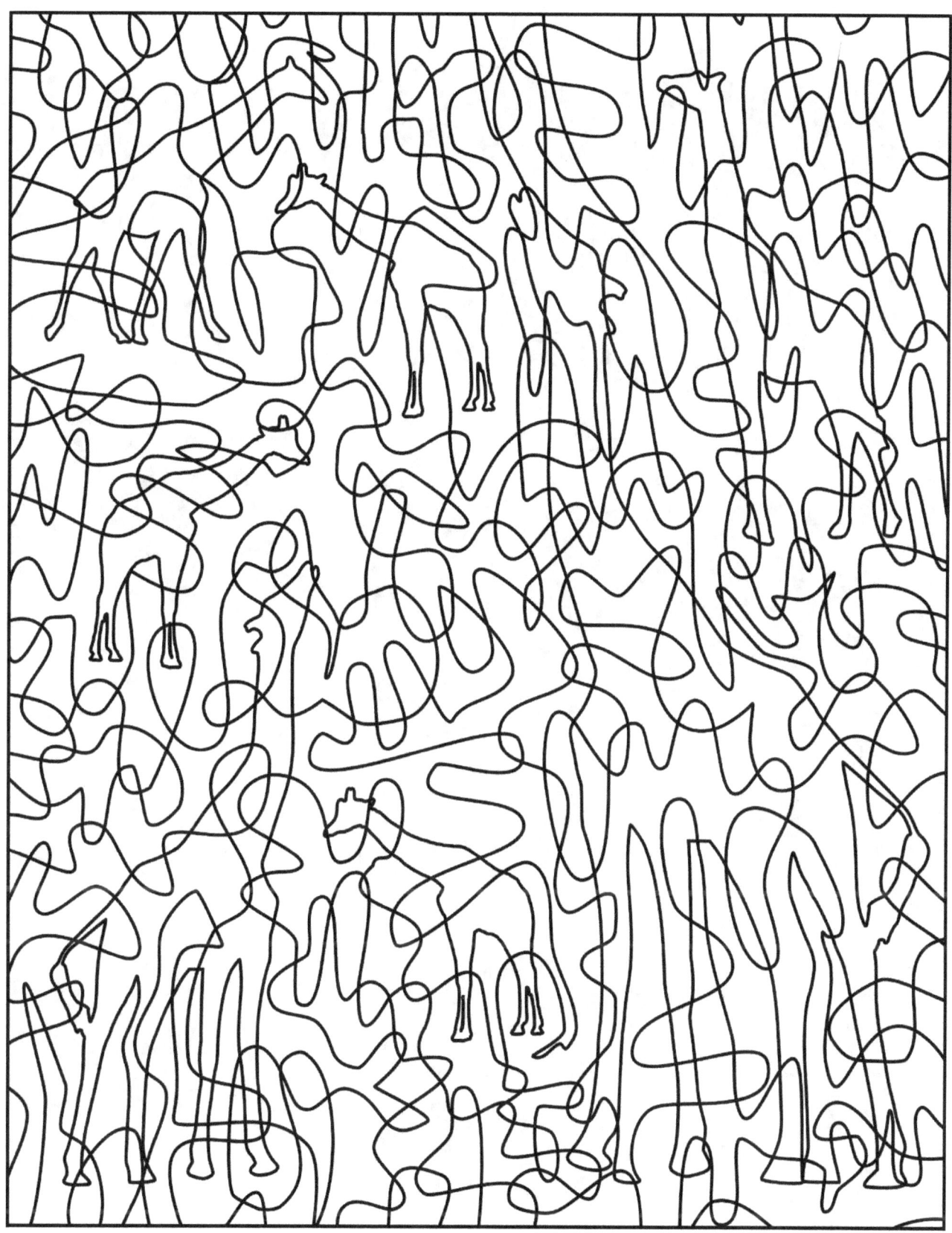

7 giraffes

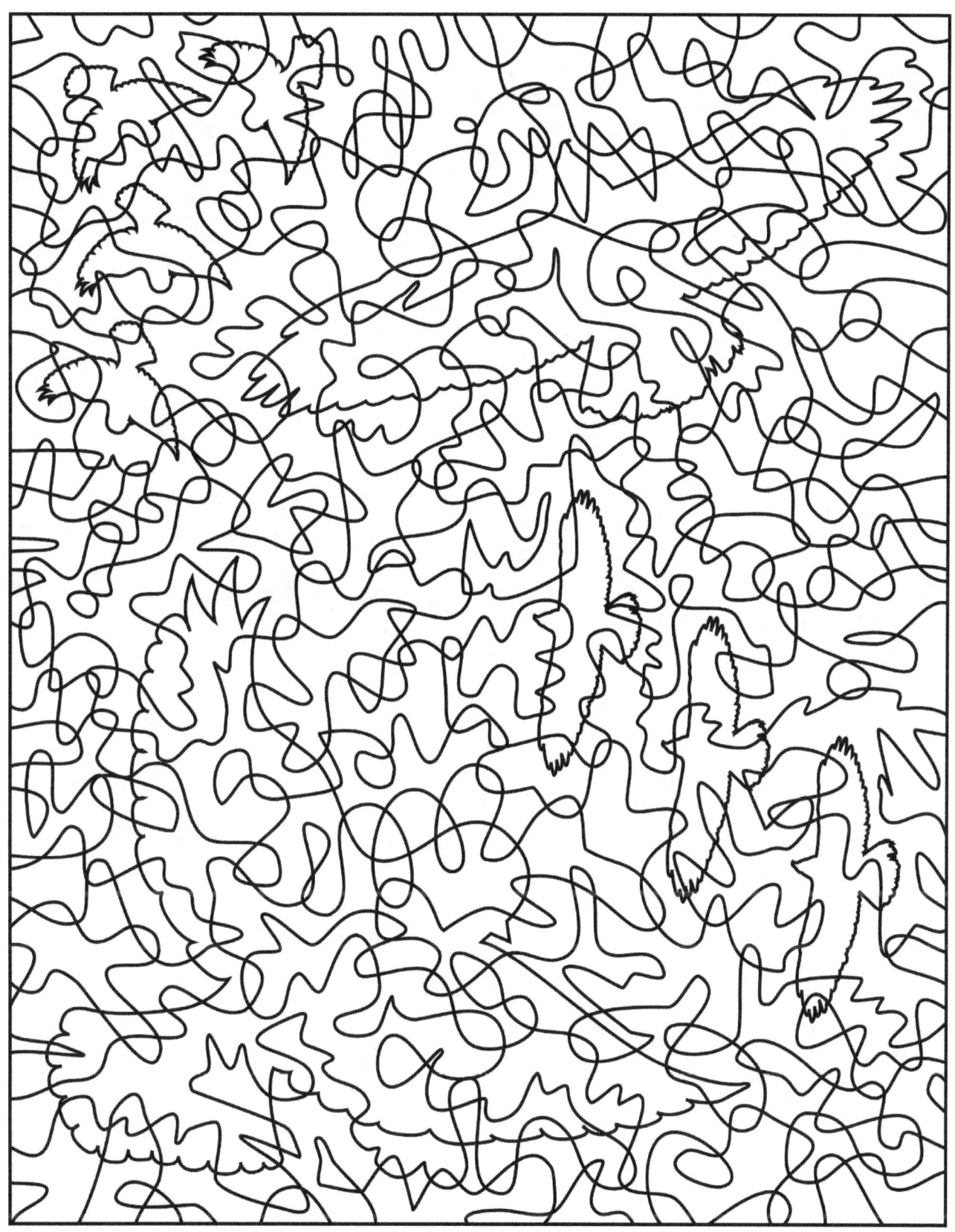

9 birds

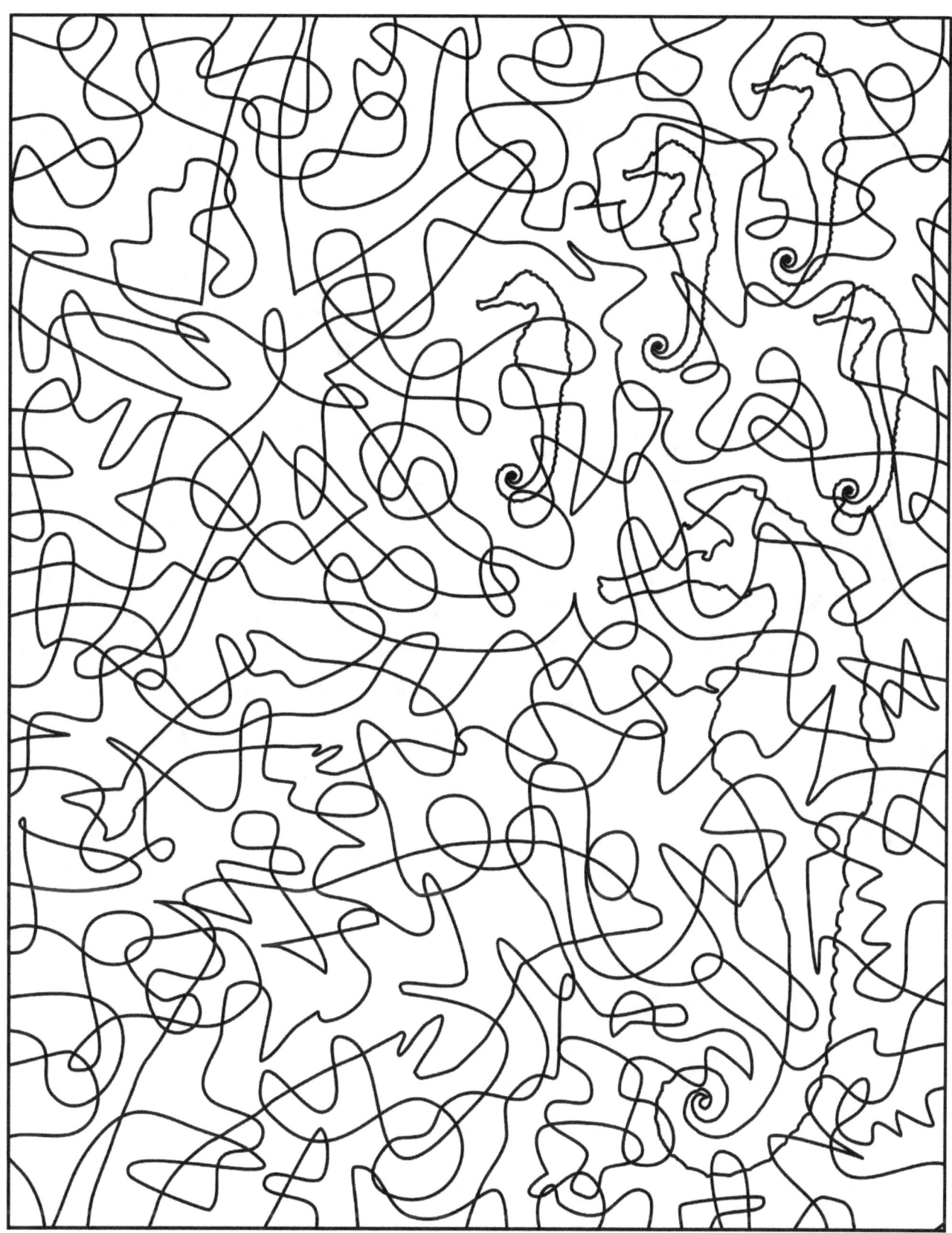

5 seahorses, 2 dolphins, 1 starfish

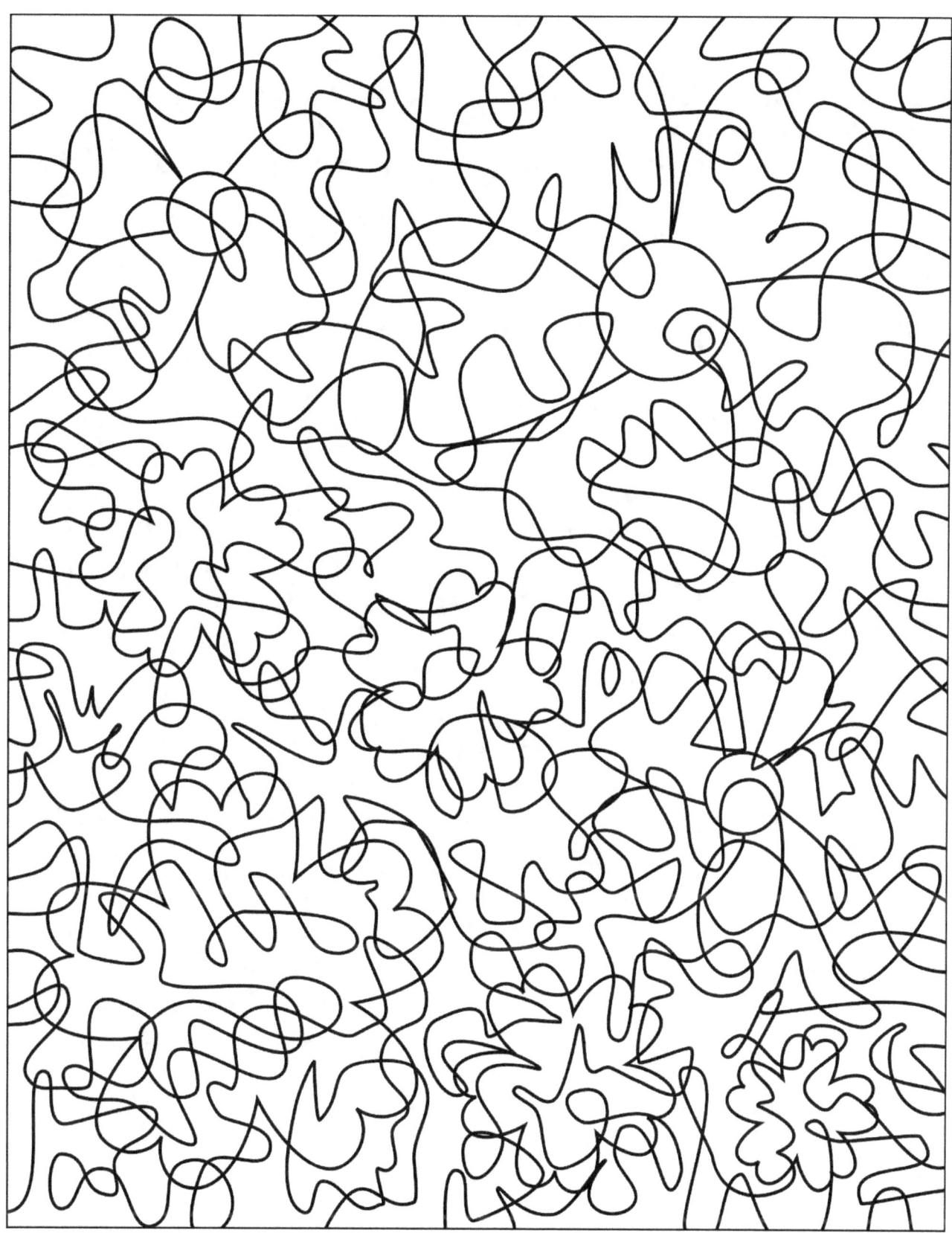

8 flowers

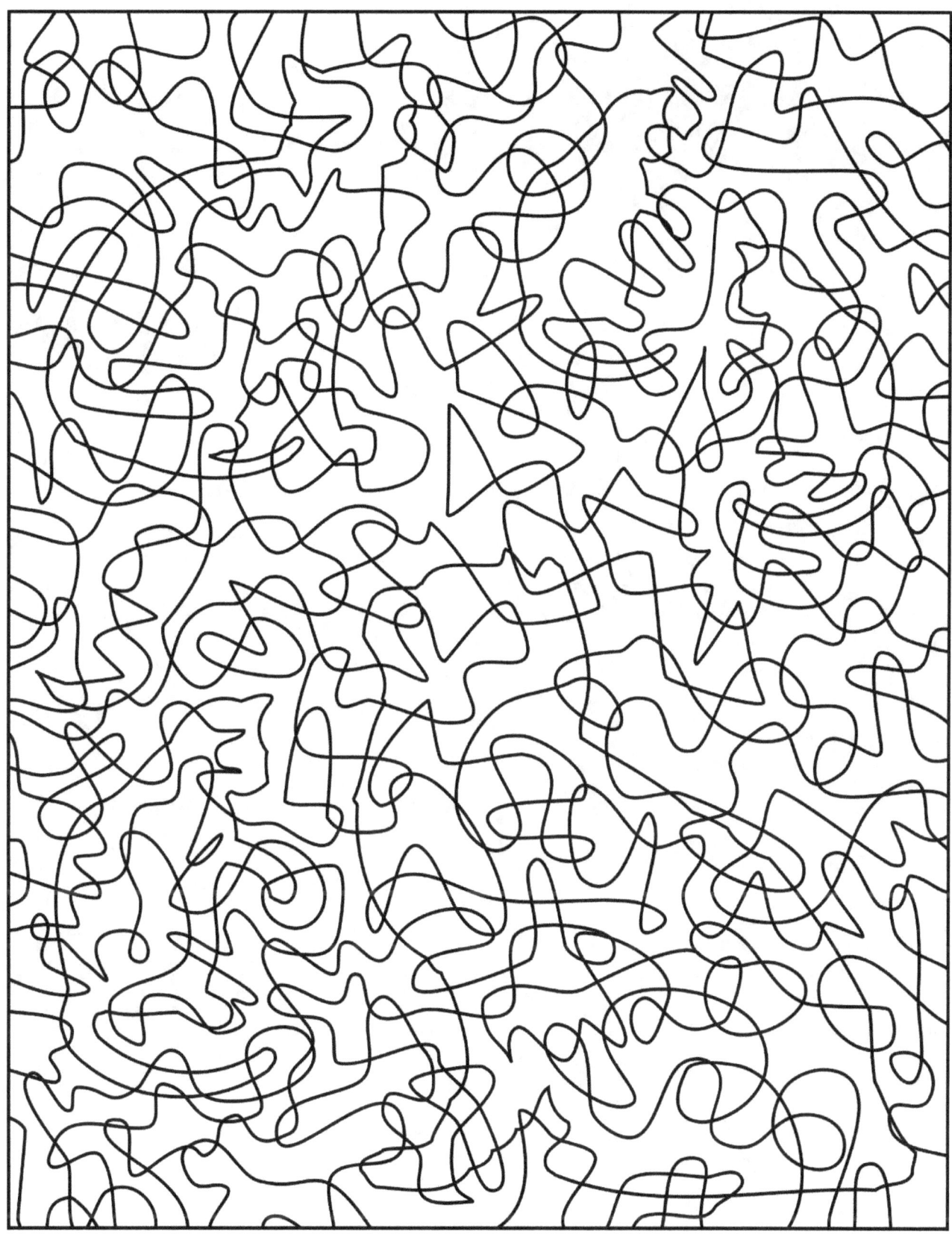

5 cats

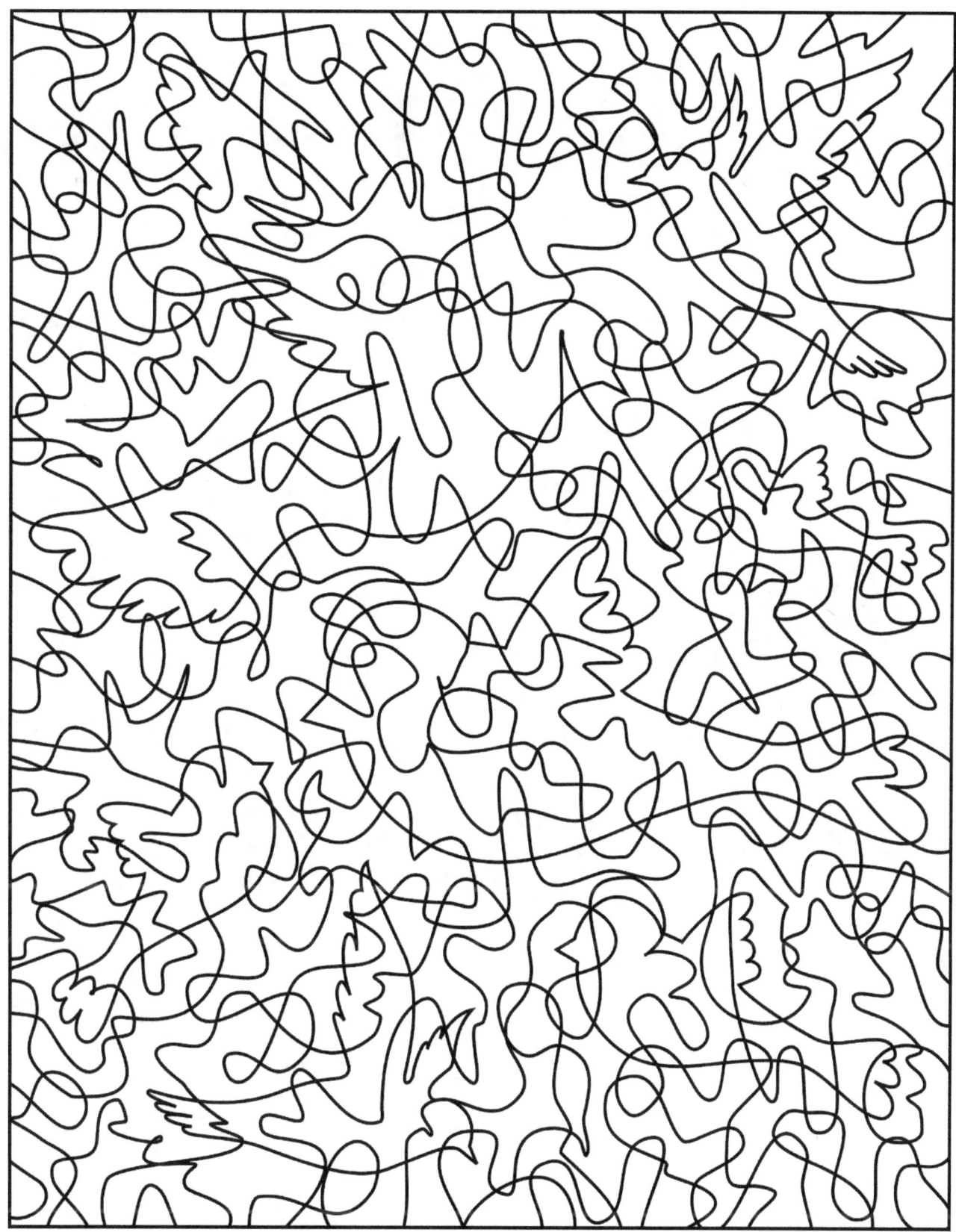

7 birds

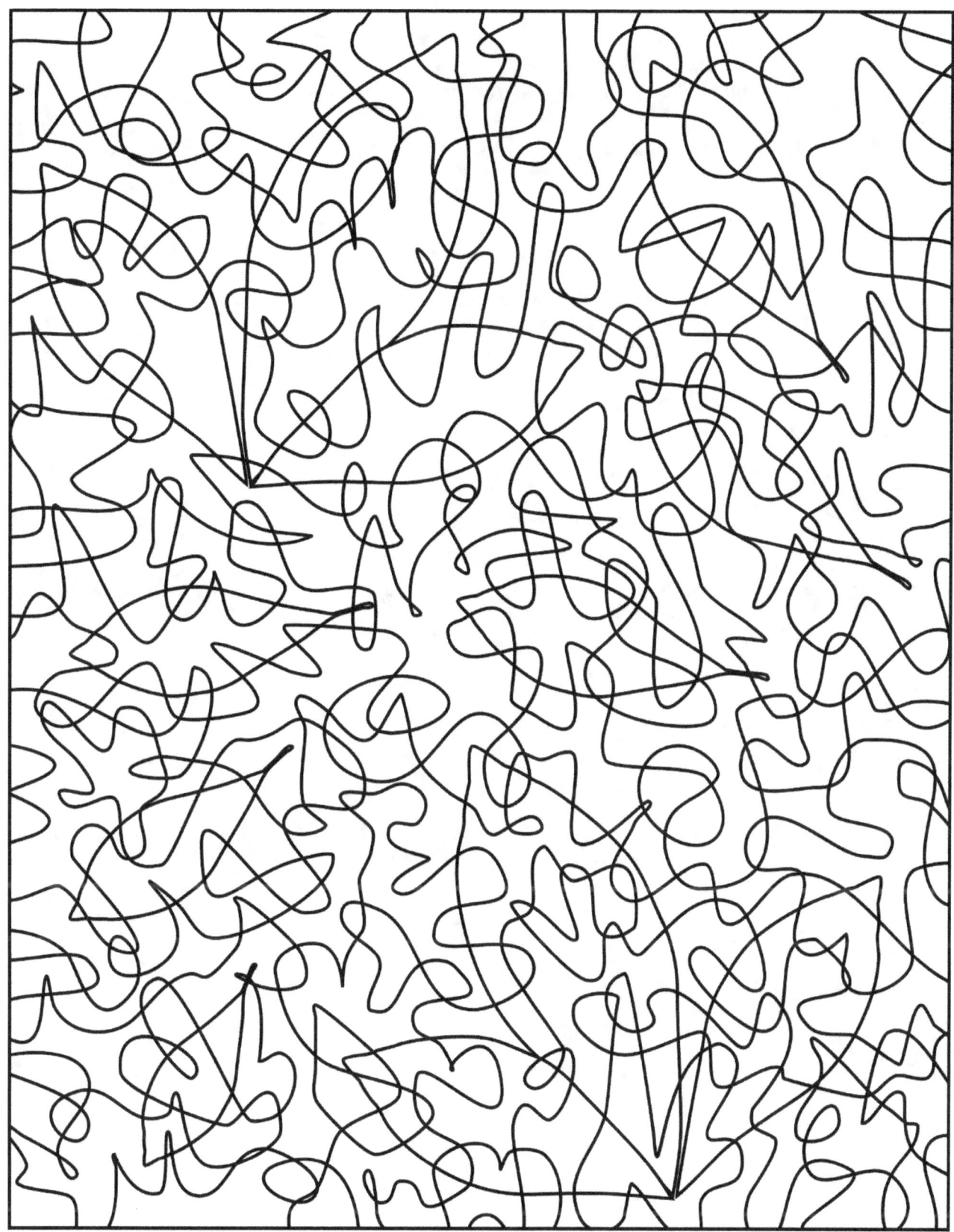

12 leaves

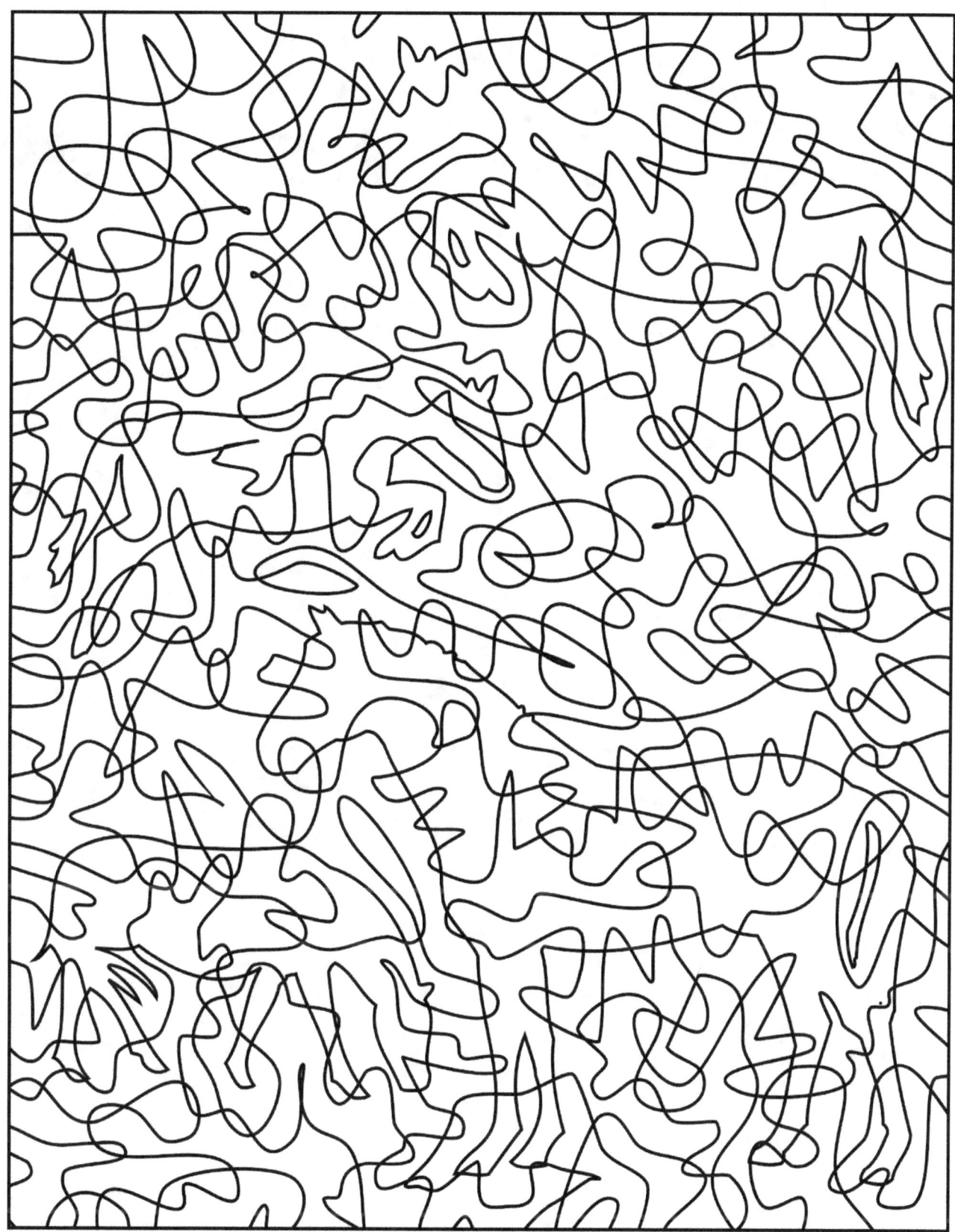

4 horses

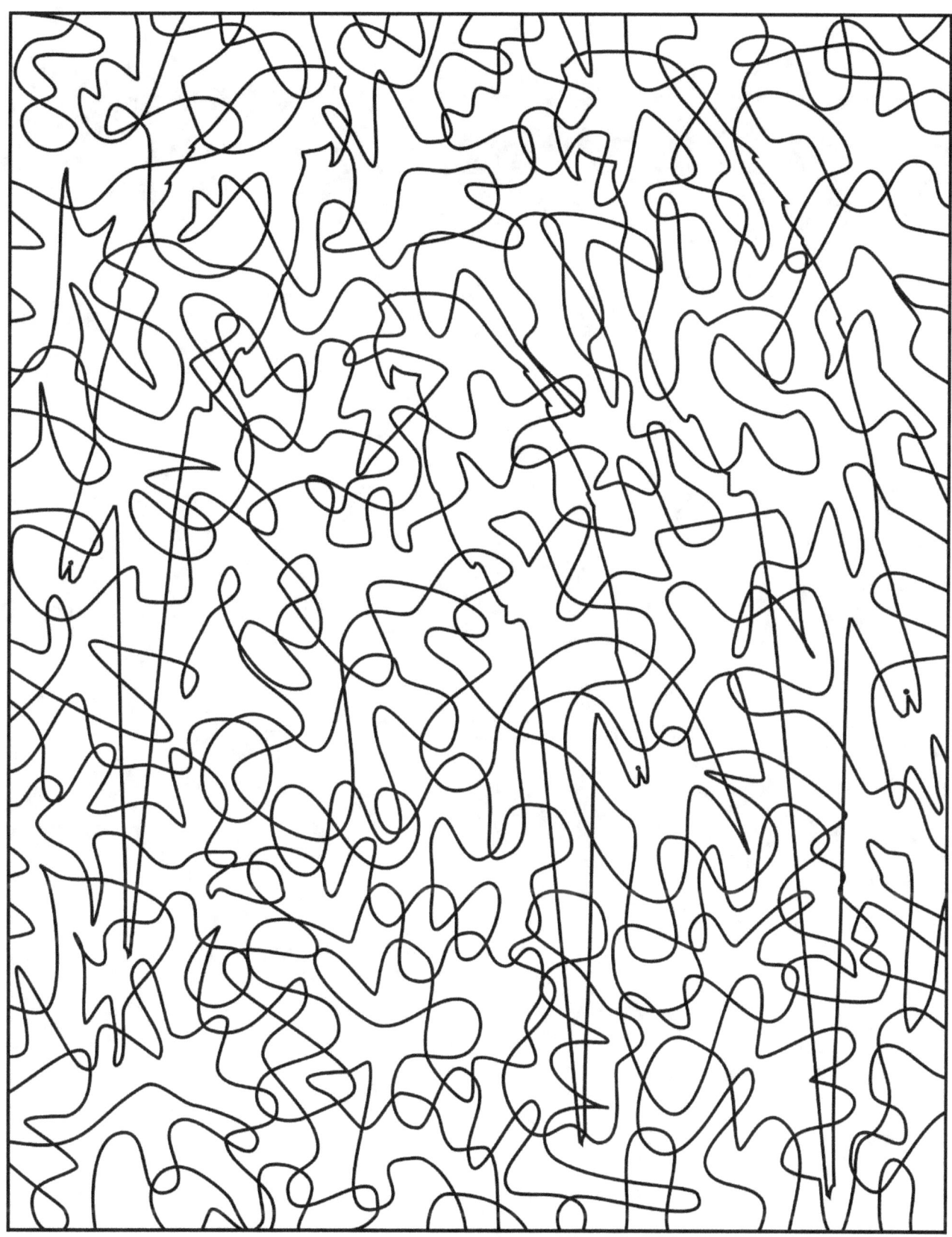

3 birds

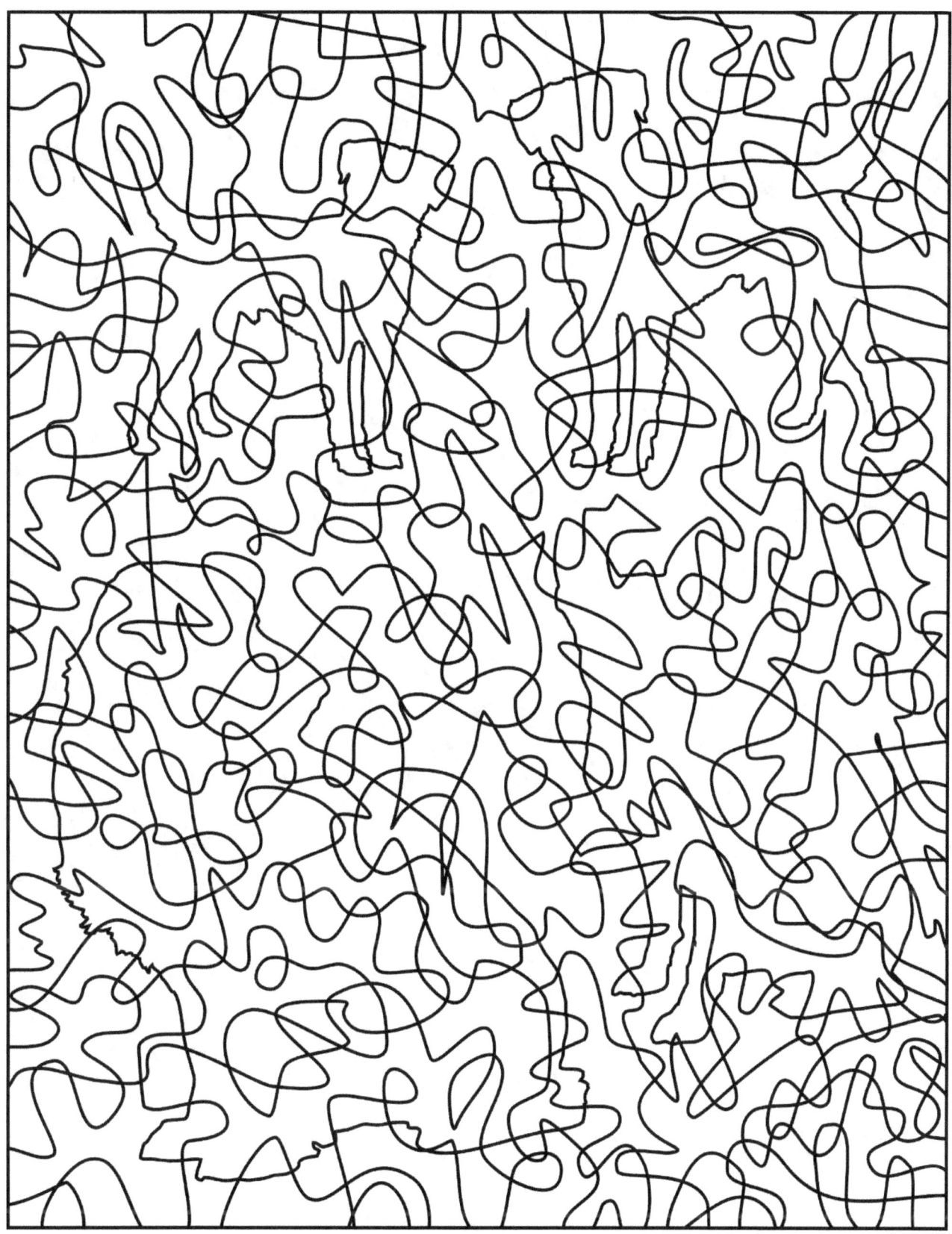

4 dogs

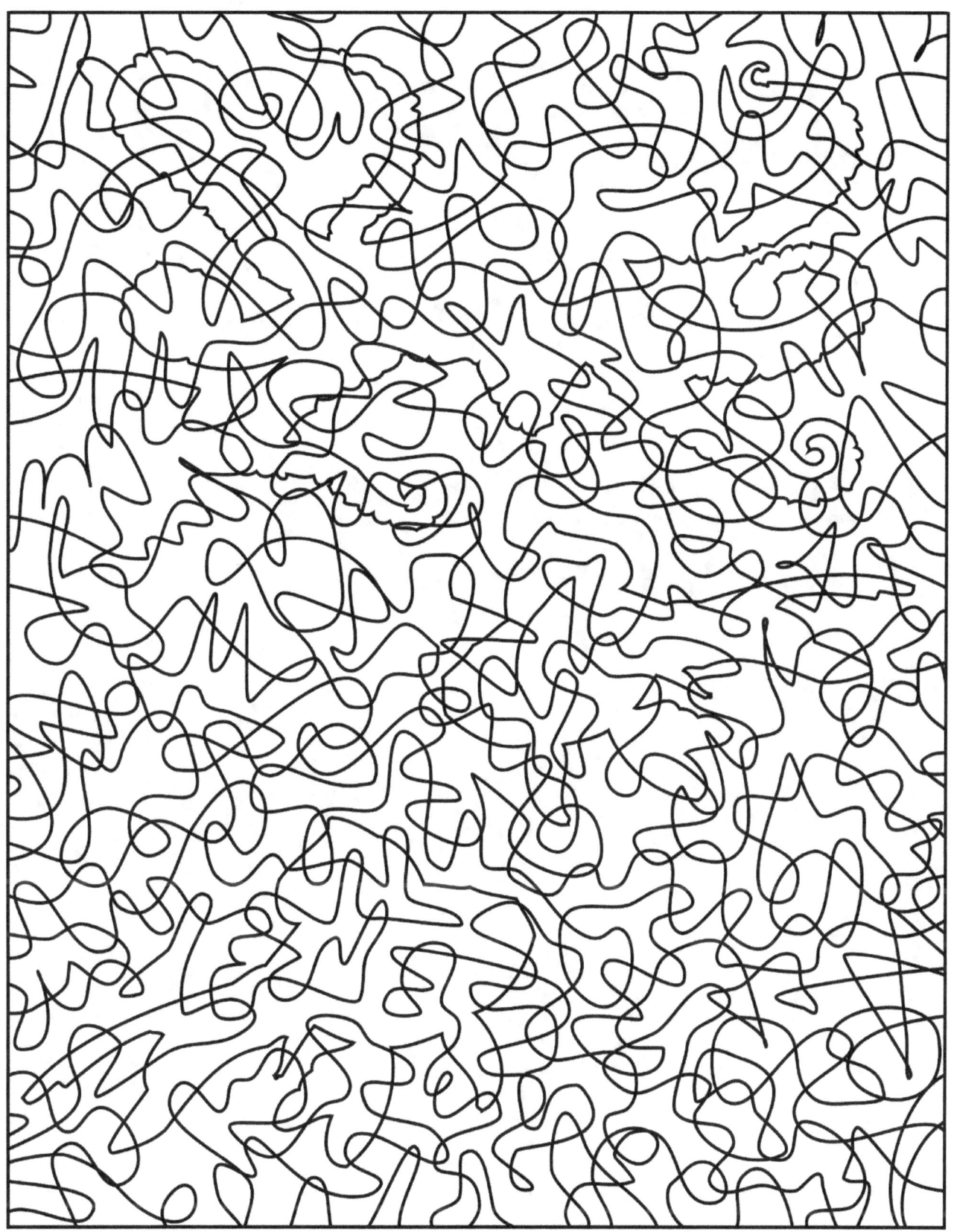

2 fish, 1 octopus

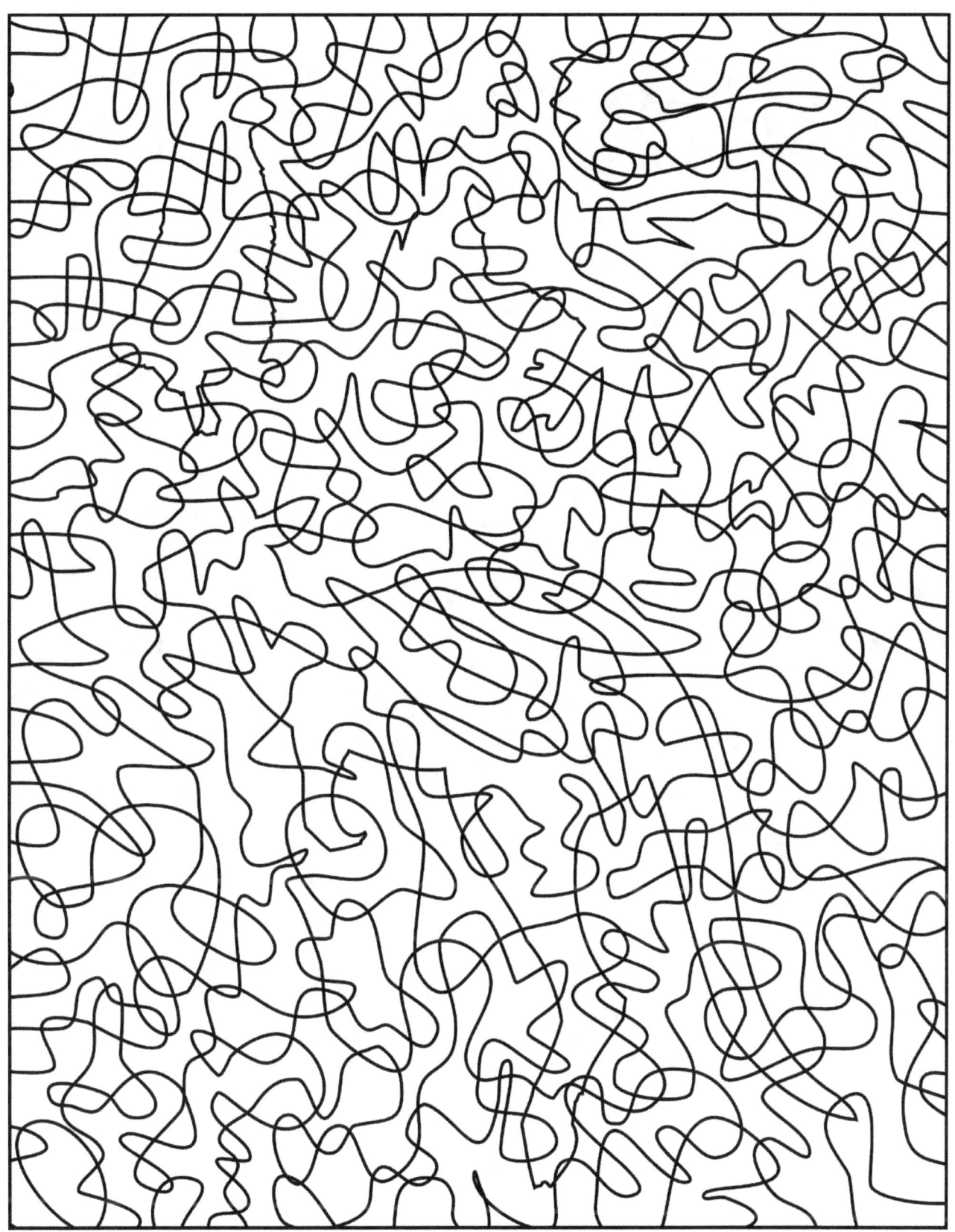

1 kangaroo, 1 meerkat, 1 lemur

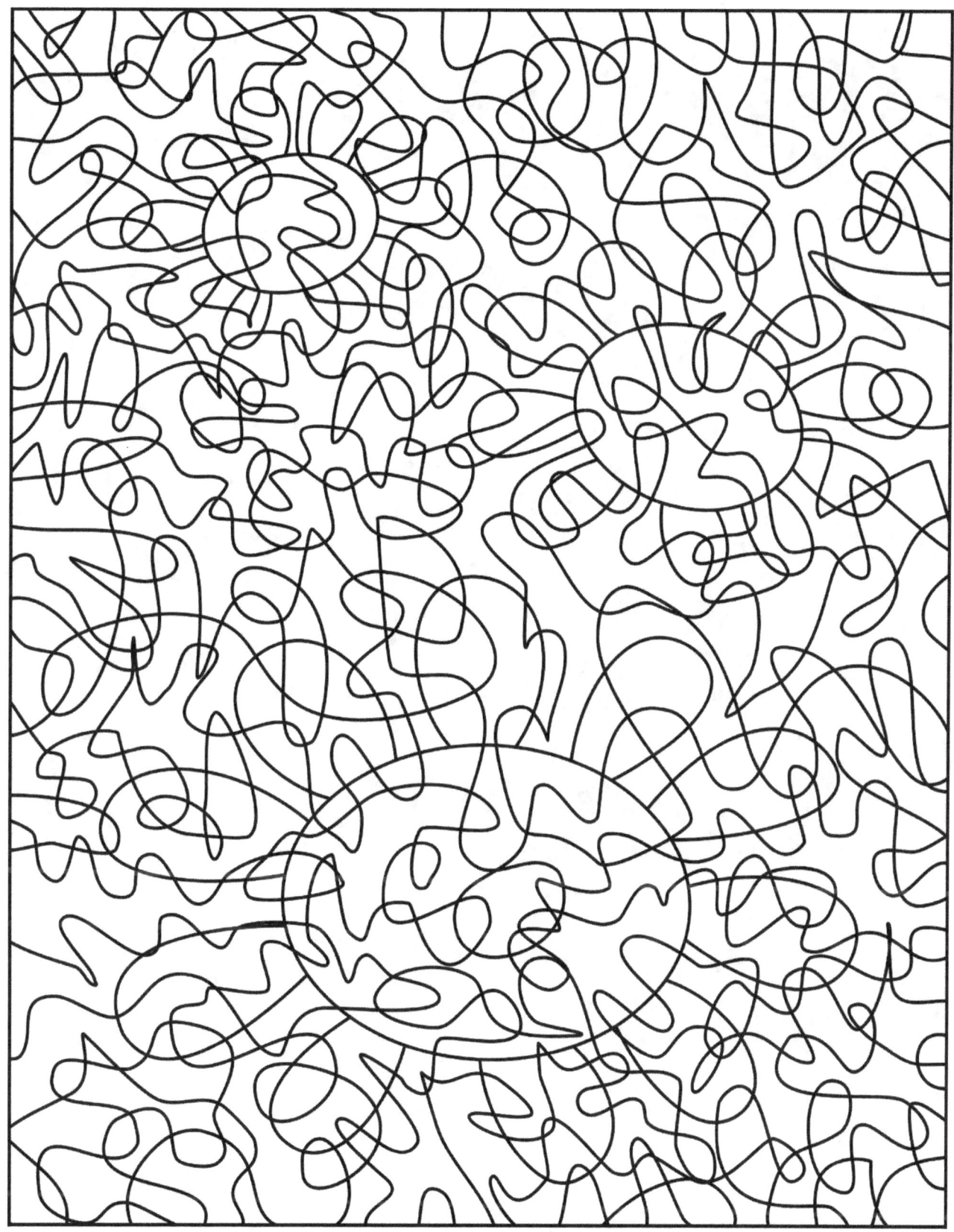

3 flowers

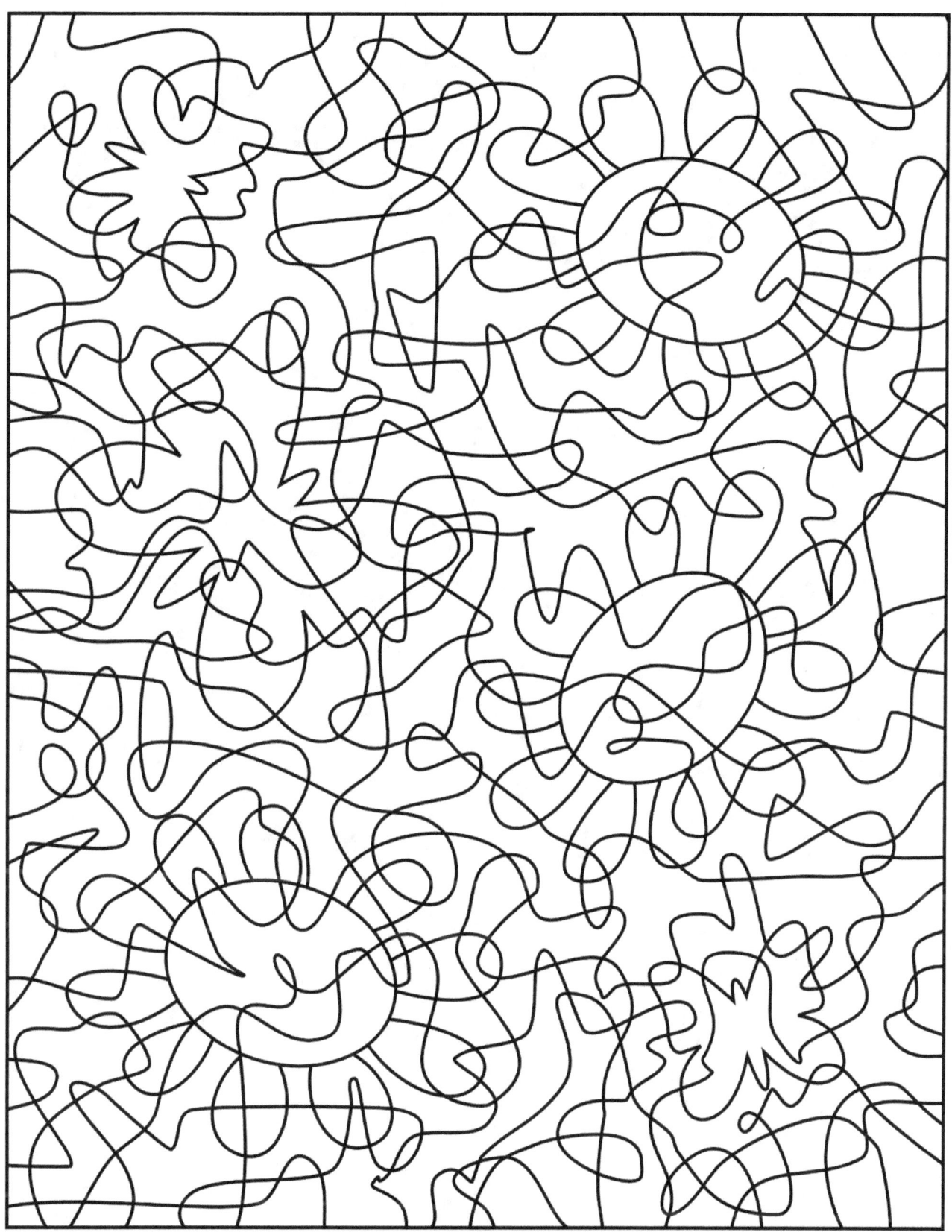

3 flowers, 3 butterflies

SOLUTIONS

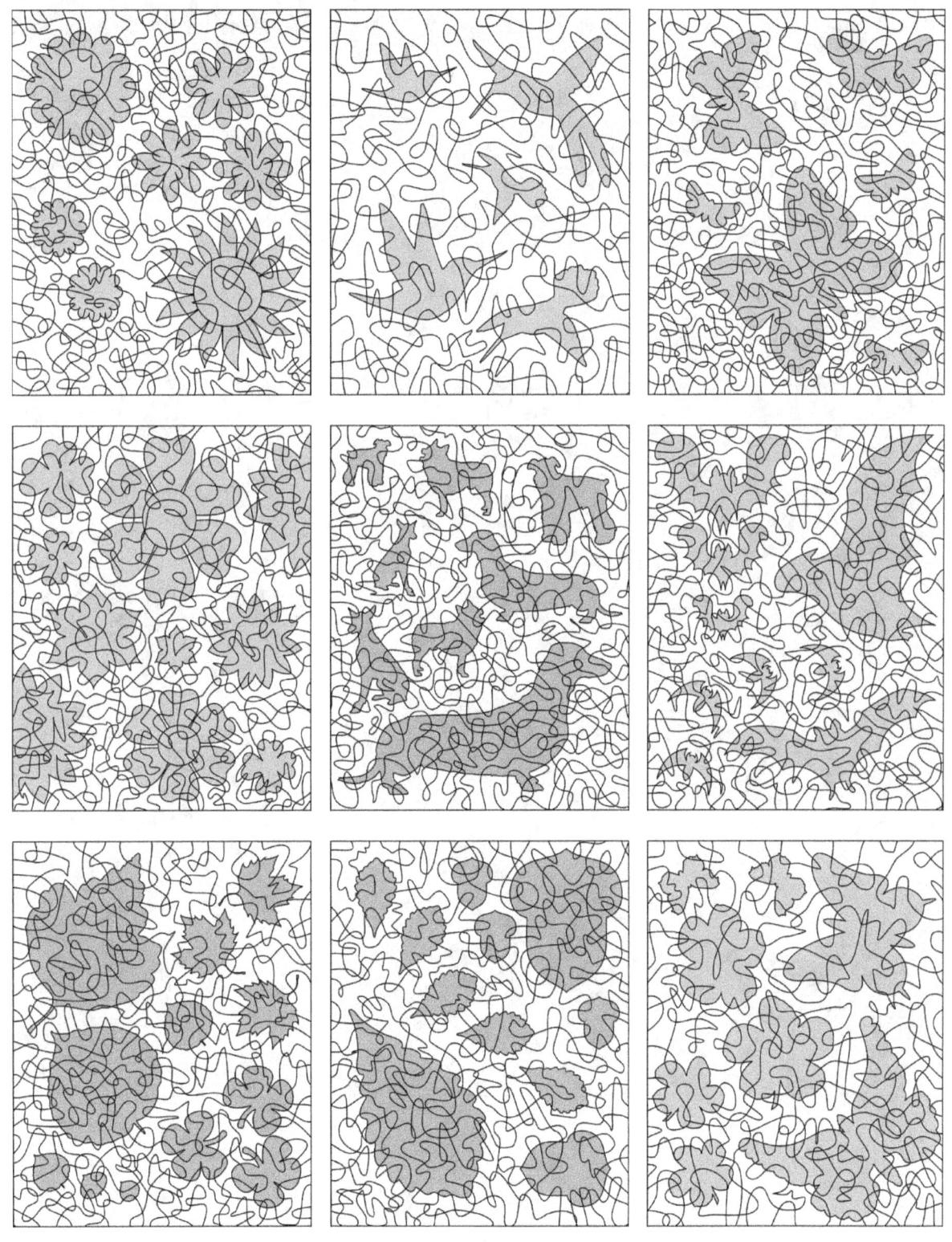

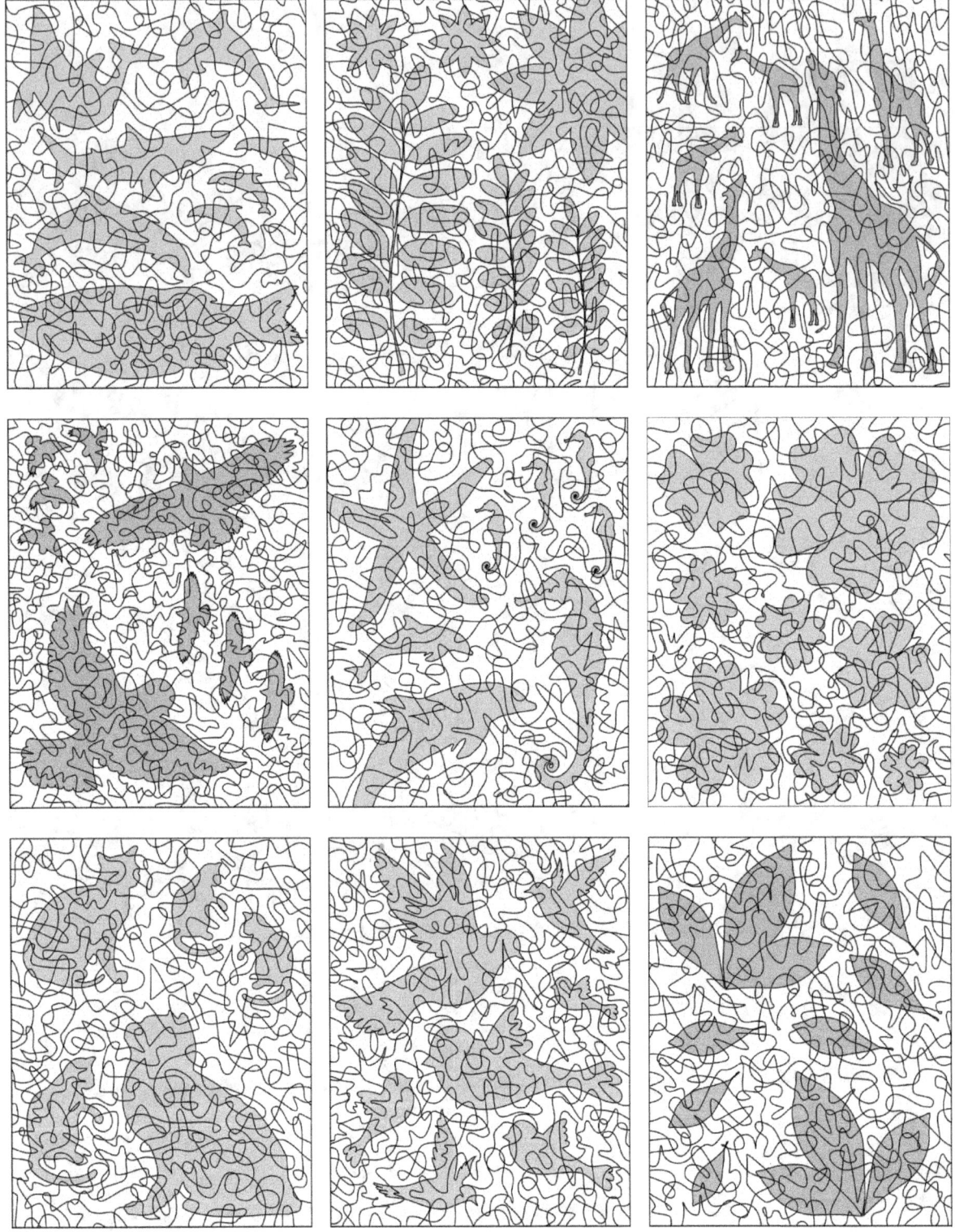

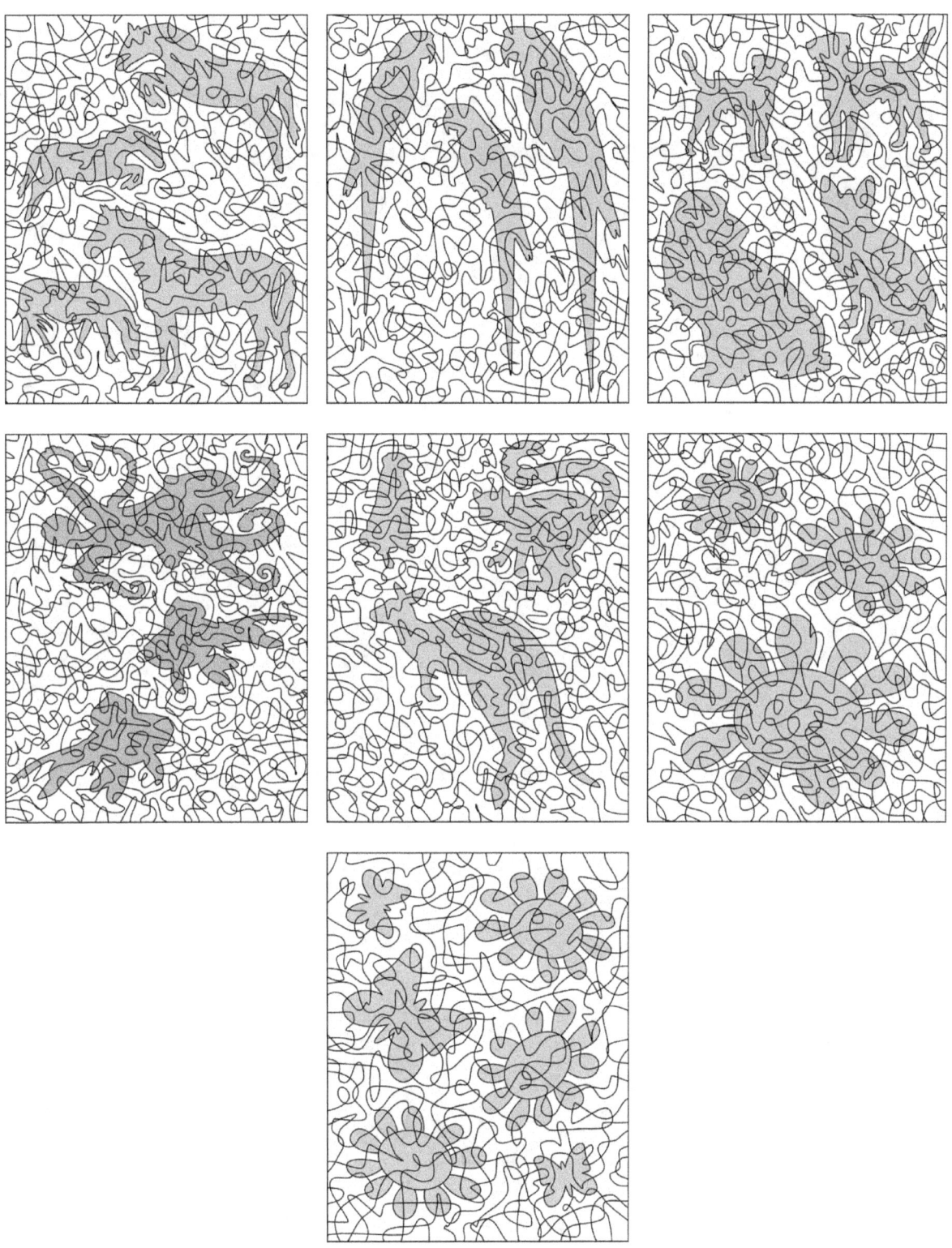

www.ingramcontent.com/pod-product-compliance
Lightning Source LLC
Chambersburg PA
CBHW081616170526
45166CB00009B/2985